Anne Elizabeth's DIARY

A Young Artist's True Story

Written and illustrated by
Anne Elizabeth Rector

with additional text by
Kathleen Krull

Megan Tingley Books

LITTLE, BROWN AND COMPANY

New York ~ Boston

To everyone who keeps a diary

— K.K.

Little, Brown and Company

Time Warner Book Group
1271 Avenue of the Americas, New York, NY 10020
Visit our Web site at www.lb-kids.com

First Edition

Library of Congress Cataloging-in-Publication Data
Rector, Anne Elizabeth.
   Anne Elizabeth's diary: a young artist's true story / written and illustrated by Anne
Elizabeth Rector ; with additional text by Kathleen Krull — 1st ed.
     p. cm.
   "Megan Tingley books."
   Summary: The diary of a twelve-year-old girl living in New York City in 1912, with
sidebars describing the author/illustrator's life and family and significant events of the
year and the city.
   ISBN 0-316-07204-4
   1. Rector, Anne Elizabeth, b. 1899 — Diaries — Juvenile literature. 2. Girls — New York
(State) — New York — Diaries — Juvenile literature. 3. Child artists — New York (State) —
New York — Diaries — Juvenile literature. 4. New York (N.Y.) — Biography — Juvenile
literature. [1. Rector, Anne Elizabeth, b. 1899. 2. Artists. 3. Women — Biography. 4. New
York (N.Y.) — Social life and customs — 20th century. 5. Diaries.] I. Krull, Kathleen. II. Title.
F128.5.R24 2004
974.7'1041'092 — dc21
[B]   2003047443

10 9 8 7 6 5 4 3 2 1

IM

Printed in China

Book design by Alyssa Morris and Sue Dennen

The illustrations for this book were done in pen-and-ink.
The text was set in Basing and Diotima, and the display
typefaces are Ballerino and Sackers.

Introduction

Meet Anne Elizabeth Rector, age twelve, a real American girl who lived almost a hundred years ago in New York City.

Anne Elizabeth was an only child, but she was never bored. She loved drawing and watching movies and chattering in class. Ice-skating thrilled her. She had problem teeth, a weakness for shoes, a healthy sense of humor when she wasn't being too judgmental, and a unique way of recording her life....

She was born in 1899 in Parkersburg, West Virginia, and grew up in the Morningside Heights neighborhood of New York City. Her father was a pioneer photographer and traveled constantly. Her mother was often busy sewing clothes.

Anne Elizabeth spent more time alone than most girls her age — a loner in a powerful, interesting family. In her twelfth year, she started observing her life in a most unusual diary.

Anne Elizabeth didn't just list daily events. She illustrated them with exquisite pen-and-ink miniatures of herself, her neighborhood and school, and lots of hats and shoes.

She was quite businesslike about her book. She almost always limited each entry to its own space—carefully within the lines. Her penmanship was perfect, as was *most* of her spelling. She kept up the diary fairly faithfully for the whole year of 1912.

Then, like many of us, she lapsed as a diary writer. Never again, as it turned out, would she write so directly about her own life.

But we know how things would turn out for Anne Elizabeth. And how important this year was going to be for her.

JANUARY 7

19 12 Spent the day making the poster.

An entry from Anne Elizabeth's actual diary

January 1, 1912

Daddy gave me all these art supplies for Christmas. Mother gave me one thing, this book. She instructed me to

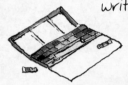

write in it every day. I shall draw here too. Mother need not know.

January 3

Mother in bed again all day. One of her sewing headaches. Went to the St. Nicholas skating rink with Daddy. It was my first time on ice and I will not say how many times I fell. We laughed a great deal.

Anne Elizabeth lived...

at 414 West 118th Street in Morningside Heights, a kind of "secret garden" in the New York City of her day. On the top northwest part of Manhattan, it is roughly bordered by 106th Street, 123rd Street, Morningside Park, and Riverside Park. From a bluff, the area overlooks the Hudson River on one side and Harlem on the other. Even as Harlem and the Upper West Side became thoroughly developed, this land remained farmland. In the mid-1800s, an unbuildable plot was set aside for a park called "Morning-side" because its hill caught the morning sun. The name rubbed off on the area. By the turn of the century, Morningside still had cottages and vegetable gardens, but it was also attracting universities and churches. These nonprofit institutions needed large sites away from the high rents and jam-packed streets of midtown Manhattan. In 1904 a new subway station opened under Broadway, the immense boulevard that runs from one end of New York to the other. Now Midtown was only twenty convenient minutes away. Middle-class apartment houses like Anne Elizabeth's began sprouting up on empty lots. The Rectors' rent was a mere $30 a month (about $555 in today's dollars). Anne Elizabeth probably had her own room, but the rest of the apartment would have been taken up by her mother's sewing business and her father's various projects.

January 4

Ah, school. I had not seen my friends in so long that I got in trouble for talking in Grammar class. Especially to Emilie, my best friend. She got her own <u>horse</u> for Christmas.

January 5

We are to have a spelling match with the seventh grade. Emilie and I spent the afternoon studying the words. I spell well, but I fear standing up in class to do it.

Ernest Thompson Seton...

was famous for having cofounded the Boy Scouts of America. Seton (1860–1946) wrote their first handbook and served as "Chief Scout" from 1910 until 1915. But he was even more famous as a naturelover. Writing and drawing, he worked tirelessly to inspire others — especially children — to discover and cherish the environment. In addition to *Wild Animals I Have Known* and many other bestselling books, Seton wrote thousands of articles as well as animal definitions and drawings for new dictionaries. He was also a dramatic storyteller and lecturer, an expert in Native-American sign language, and an early supporter of the political rights of American Indians. He called himself "Black Wolf."

January 6

In front of the entire art class, Miss Pratt asked me to make a poster. It is for a lecture by Ernest Thompson Seton, who is coming to our school. She chose me out of all the good artists in class. Daddy gave me the paper to make it on.

January 8

Working on poster. Daddy came back from his trip tonight, and I had to ask him to help me with my arithmetic, not my best subject.

January 9

Still postering. I asked Daddy to go skating, but he was packing for another trip. I feel I never see him.

January 10

We won the spelling match. I did not make a fool of myself.

January 11

Had a piano lesson, spent rest of the day on poster. I do like drawing much more than writing, even in my diary. Mother still does not know I draw pictures here.

Anne Elizabeth's school…

was in an imposing building, complete with a doorman, on West 120th Street in her neighborhood of Morningside Heights. Thanks to money from wealthy donors, the Horace Mann School had electricity and whatever equipment and supplies it needed. A large statue of Athena, the Greek goddess of wisdom, greeted everyone in the front hallway. During Anne Elizabeth's time, the teachers lived across the street, in a building that was formerly the Bloomingdale Insane Asylum. Otherwise the area was country-like, with geese and goats wandering across empty lots.

The school was named for Horace Mann (1796–1859), a crusader for mandatory public school education in America. At first the school was an experiment for education students affiliated with the Teachers College of Columbia University. The college was the birthplace of progressive education in America, using fresh ideas from philosopher John Dewey. The first four students at Horace Mann were two sets of siblings. Within a few years, the school included all grade levels from nursery school to high school. Boys and girls were taught separately — reading, writing, math, science, visual and performing arts, plus sports. The school had athletic teams for both girls and boys. In addition to academics, report cards graded lung capacity, forearm strength, and hand-eye coordination.

January 12

Took my poster to school and Miss Pratt said it was wonderfully clever. I think other girls were jealous.

January 13

After school, went shopping with Nannie. I suppose many girls are closer to their grandmothers than their mothers. Found a coat I like very much. It is reversible, but I wear it on the dark blue side with the light blue collar.

Anne Elizabeth with Nannie

January 14

Daddy took me skating up at Van Cortlandt and I did very much better. I do wish I could see him every day, or that he would take me on his travels.

Anne Elizabeth's father, Enoch Rector

Anne Elizabeth's parents,
Jessie (seated) and Enoch Rector, with friend

Anne Elizabeth's father,...

Enoch Rector, was a pioneer photographer whose work led him to travel constantly. When he was home, he made a point of taking Anne Elizabeth to plays and movies. He himself made the first moving picture longer than one minute — he built the camera and ground his own lenses.

January 17

Went to see "The First Lady in the Land" to celebrate Daddy's birthday. It was a little flat to suit me. The woman who played the part of Dolly Madison gave the impression of a common witty person.

January 18

Liked Mr. Seton's lecture quite well. Miss Pratt introduced me and gave him my poster. He seemed most impressed. He went to art school here in the city and can draw the most splendid animals.

January 19

Geography and Mathematics tests in the morning. I could not have done very well. I can not help fearing I will never graduate from Horace Mann.

January 20

In the afternoon I played outdoors by myself. Sisters would be lovely to have. Sometimes Daddy says he wishes he had sons. Even brothers could be good companions.

Anne Elizabeth, only child

January 21

Daddy took Emilie and me to Van Cortlandt. It is as splendid to draw skaters as to skate away on an icy cold day.

January 22

For the first time, Mother came skating with us. We had a glorious time.

Baby Anne Elizabeth with her mother

January 23

Mother ill today. Went to see "Ben Hur" with Nannie. We thought it was the best play we had seen all year. I wore my new coat. I hope Nannie will always be my special friend.

Toys of Anne Elizabeth's time…

were usually homemade. Those who could afford them bought dolls, which had been mass-produced in America for about fifty years. Talking dolls had been around since 1887, when inventor Thomas Edison helped to create them. Other common toys were tin soldiers, farm animals made of lead, kaleidoscopes, dollhouses, alphabet blocks, and puppets. Lionel toy trains, Crayola crayons (in eight colors), and teddy bears (named for the popular president and animal lover Theodore Roosevelt) had all been around for about ten years. Ouija boards, chess, and card games of all kinds were popular. On the horizon were Lincoln Logs, erector sets, Radio Flyer wagons, and a cloth doll with yarn hair named Raggedy Ann.

January 24

Went over to Emilie's before my piano lesson. We played with her dolls, but we are getting too big for them, I am sad to say.

January 26

For the first time in my life I have gotten 100% on a Mathematics test. I also got 100% in Grammar. I could tell Mother was happy. She bought me a pretty new hat and muff to celebrate.

January 27

Went with Miss Robbins, our upstairs neighbor, to a gallery exhibition of "Old Masters." I loved the peasant woman with a Dutch cap and big ruff.

January 28

Daddy is gone again. I miss him.
In the evening, Mrs. Vanderbilt had
Sunday tea with us. She is one of
Mother's best sewing customers.
I poured the tea and then
sketched all evening.

New York Pleasures, Part II

Another advantage of life in the city is the lively art
scene. New York was the artistic capital of the
nation by the 1870s. Artists from all over the world
vied to show their work in its galleries and muse-
ums, seeking the approval of its educated, sophisti-
cated population. Galleries at this time preferred
European art over American, and older art over
newer styles. New Yorkers were about to be
shocked by the infamous Armory Show, which
arrived in 1913 and introduced them to post-
impressionism and cubism. Well-known artists
working at this time included Pablo Picasso, Marc
Chagall, Henri Matisse, Vassili Kandinsky, Paul Klee,
Georges Braque, and Pierre Auguste Renoir.

Clothes during this time . . .

could be purchased in brand-new
department stores, but wealthier
Americans still hired seamstresses.
Thousands of women like Anne
Elizabeth's mother cut fabric using
patterns of the latest fashions
supplied by women's magazines,
creating made-to-order clothes for
customers who paid them directly.
They were able to support them-
selves at home in a respectable
way. Others — poor immigrant
workers who weren't so lucky —
worked in factories that supplied
clothes to stores. The era was
unenlightened about the conditions in factories, which were bru-
tal enough to cause injury or
death. Workers had no rights. A
year earlier, in 1911, the worst factory fire in the history of New York
broke out at a shirt factory. Some
500 women worked at the Triangle
Shirtwaist Company under miser-
able conditions, fifteen hours
every day for wages of $6 to $8 a
week. To keep workers from steal-
ing supplies, doors were kept
locked. So when the fire started,
not everyone was able to evacu-
ate, and 146 young women
jumped out the windows to their
deaths. The tragedy led New York
to form the Bureau of Fire to
enforce factory fire regulations,
and it galvanized the movement
for workers' rights.

January 29

Mother washed my hair. While it was drying, she said if I spent more time on school, instead of drawing, I would always get 100% on my tests.

January 30

While I was making sandwiches for Mother's lunch, we battled again. Cut my finger so I could not practice piano. So I went over to Emilie's and spent the afternoon. Emilie never argues with her mother.

January 31

My finger was better so I had a music lesson. But practicing piano is like a duty. When I am drawing I lose all track of time.

February 1, 1912

There was a man calling strawberries in the street today. Spring must be coming. Miss Pratt has told me about a special art class near Cape Cod this summer. She wants me to attend. Mother would never agree.

Streets in New York, Part I

Vendors selling all sorts of items, especially fresh produce, on trays or pushcarts would stroll the streets of New York City. For new immigrants, carts were a way to start their own businesses — a portable store. This was a time when immigrants were pouring into America. Nine years earlier, the Statue of Liberty had been inscribed with an invitation to the world's homeless. Millions, mostly from countries in Europe, accepted. As many as 20,000 people a day were being inspected and registered at New York's Ellis Island. Those who stayed on in the city typically went to the overcrowded slums of the Lower East Side.

February 2

Started my Valentines today. Made Emilie's first. Made a large one for Miss Pratt for telling me about the art class. Still too afraid to ask Mother.

February 3

Went skating and saw a baby on skates. He was about two and a half years old. Darling. I love children, though it is hard to imagine my own, as everyone tells me I will have.

February 4

Mother is sick, and the whole house is downcast. I fear she has been working over much. She is an artist with clothes, but the work tires her.

February 6

Mother is better. Their friends came over to play bridge. They said I was not old enough to play, so I sketched. Daddy is going to teach me chess.

February 9

Went downtown with Mother to buy shoes. Had luncheon with Nannie at the Arts Club. Went skating with Daddy. I told _all_ of them about the art class on the Cape this summer, but no one seemed very interested.

New York Pleasures, Part III

One of the perks about life in New York is getting the best in food. Restaurants of all kinds were multiplying in Anne Elizabeth's day, with new recipes influenced by new immigrants. Women, especially if unaccompanied by men, usually weren't welcome at restaurants, men's clubs, and bars, so some wealthy women formed their own, members-only clubs. Anne Elizabeth was able to eat at social clubs like the Arts Club (for artistic men and women) and the Cosmopolitan Club (for women). These were places where ladies could play bridge, hear lectures, or have an elegant tea. Chicken à la king might be served, with a delectable dessert such as saltines with cream cheese and cherry jelly with almonds in place of the pits.

February 10

Mother chaperoned me downtown to Laura Freeman's party. I had a beautiful time. On the way home we talked about  the art class. Mother said all ladies should be artistic and they do not need special classes.

February 12

Lincoln's Birthday. No holiday at school, but we were excused from homework. Daddy took me skating at Van Cortlandt. The ice is starting to melt. I am sorry to say he agreed with Mother about the art class.

February 13

A lovely letter from Mr. Seton thanking me for the poster I made for him. His words about my work made me blush. I showed it to Laura Freeman. She brought over her roller skates and we had lots of fun skating and then playing paper dolls.

♥ February 14

A splendid Valentine's party at Nancy's. They had a real magician come and amuse us. Art is like magic for me. I hope Mother will come around.

February 16

Was asked over to Miss Pratt's. Her niece is a very nice little girl. Miss Pratt told me more about the art class this summer. It is in Gloucester, a lovely town right on the sea. I must find a way to get Mother to let me go.

February 17

Today I wore my new woolen dress. It is a brown challis with a yellow lined collar and cuffs embroidered in brown. Mother got it to fit perfectly. Another battle about the art class. She does not think we have the extra money. I said I could stop piano lessons.

Interest in fashion…

was as high then as now. Often by way of Paris, New York set the fashion trends for the rest of America. Lavish hats with feathers and flowers were all the rage, and zippers were coming into use. For the daring, necklines were lowering and hemlines were rising. Pink was popular, as were dresses with narrow waists. Skirts could be slim enough as to inhibit movement. These so-called "hobble skirts" were so easy to rip that women took to binding their legs together with cord to prevent normal steps, or else cutting slits to allow for easier movement. A variation on the hobble skirt was the peg skirt. This was cut much fuller at the top than at the bottom, giving a woman the appearance of carrying saddlebags on her hips.

February 18

Went for a walk with Daddy. He said the oddest thing, that ladies should not go to school too much, that men do not approve. It is getting warm rapidly. I saw a man selling flowers on the street.

February 19

Tea with Miss Pratt at the Cosmopolitan Club. She is sailing to Egypt with her Father. Mother said the art class was more than we could afford. But Miss Pratt might arrange for me to pay less than the other girls.

Travel by ship…

was the way people got to other countries during this time. (Not until 1928 did commercial airline flight begin.) Ships were getting increasingly luxurious, more like floating hotels. Two months from now, on April 15, 1912, the largest passenger ship in the world would set sail to New York on its first voyage. The glamorous vessel was said by everyone to be unsinkable. But the *Titanic* would hit an iceberg on its way, and it would sink. More than 1,500 people, including some prominent New Yorkers, would die in the freezing Atlantic Ocean.

February 20

Miss Pratt set sail this morning, and Mother and I went down to see her off. I will miss her so much. No one is as kind to me. Mother never praises me. She believes giving praise is bad manners.

February 21

Went to class party. I decorated all the refreshments. Scrumptious. Except that Emilie told me some of the girls think I am too conceited.

February 22

The Vanderbilt baby is the sweetest thing I ever saw. Began to make a baby book for Mrs. Vanderbilt, while Mother sewed new dresses for her. What I like best about babies are their playthings.

Young Anne Elizabeth

February 24

Nannie was off to Philadelphia to visit our cousins. I walked her to the carriage. Nannie does not think art school is for girls, but that if I really want to go, she will help. I know I am being stubborn.

February 26

Emilie and I played hopscotch. It poured rain so we came in and had cocoa. She finds me odd for wanting to go to school in the summer. But then, she is not so fond of school.

The rights of women...

were few and far between during this time. Women's wages were always lower, males were free to bully women workers, and most colleges refused to admit women. A 1908 U.S. Supreme Court ruling referred to their biological "inferiority." Not until 1920 would women win suffrage (the right to vote), and many were violently opposed to the idea in 1912, including some influential women and religious figures. Politicians insisted that women would lose charm and delicacy if they got involved, and it was even common to link women's wanting to vote to mental illness.

A few bright spots: Some 20,000 suffrage supporters joined a New York City parade this year, gaining publicity amid the half million onlookers, not all of them friendly. (In 1913, at President Woodrow Wilson's inauguration in Washington, marchers for suffrage were spat on, slapped, and poked with cigars by angry men.) Also in 1912, Juliette Gordon Low founded the Girl Scouts of the U.S.A., an organization to send girls into the outdoors, encourage their self-reliance and resourcefulness, and prepare them for more varied roles as adult women.

February 29

After piano lesson, I played
with the daughter of one of Mother's
customers. Children are a lot of trouble,
but I do love little girls who still like to
play paper dolls.

March 3, 1912

Drew a page called "The Arrival" for my Vanderbilt baby
book. It is a stork with a baby in its beak, flying over
Morningside. Comical.

March 8

Still working on my book. Played hopscotch. Ah, more signals
of Spring!

March 9

Worked on my baby book, then went for a walk
with Daddy on the aqueduct road. I ran most of
the way. Usually he does not praise, but today he said I can
run as well as any boy. I like it when he says I am the next
best thing to a son.

March 10

Mother in bed all day. Mrs. Vanderbilt's cousin is getting married,
and they have asked Mother to sew dresses for the wedding. It
is a great deal of work, but also a great deal of money.

March 12

Emilie's birthday. I made her a card and we
played paper dolls. I hope I am never too old for
paper dolls. I think Emilie already is.

March 13

Today I painted a picture for an exhibit going on to another
school. My new art teacher, Miss Dement, chose only a few girls
to do this. She said Miss Pratt talked to her about me.

Women artists...

who achieved fame were rare in Anne Elizabeth's time. One of the few was Mary Cassatt (1845–1926), famous as a painter of mothers and children. It was rumored that Cassatt's father said he would rather see her dead than become an artist. She left her baffled family behind in Philadelphia and found acceptance and fame in Paris. Friends told her that sticking to mother-and-child themes — never before painted except in a religious way — would most likely win her recognition. Cassatt expressed no interest in being a wife or mother. She supported women's right to vote, and urged women to become more active in government.

Meanwhile, Georgia O'Keeffe (1887–1986) came to New York from Wisconsin and Texas. She studied at Columbia University, right in Anne Elizabeth's neighborhood, from 1914 to 1916. Fiercely independent, she swirled herself in black capes and painted large. Her paintings of flowers were an acceptable subject for a woman, but her bleached animal bones caused more of a stir. As soon as she had the money (a group of her paintings sold for the highest sum paid to an American artist up to that time), she moved permanently to the desert in New Mexico.

March 18

Nannie took me to the Spring Academy to see portraits. I enjoyed very much a mother and child. Nannie pointed out that all great artists were men.

March 19

This is what Miss Dement is having us copy for Easter. I myself think it to be rather <u>silly</u>. Anyone could do it. I do like Miss Pratt better.

March 20

Went to see a wonderful Gainsborough portrait of the Duchess of Cumberland and Count Rumford. Mother bought me new shoes. She does not want to take on the Vanderbilt wedding. She fears it will be the death of her.

March 21

Prepared for a Geography test, then worked on my baby book.
It is snowing and sleeting and altogether very disagreeable.
Mother ill all day. Everyone in the house seems upset.

March 23

I must keep scarce, with Mother still in bed. Played
handball with balloons in the school Courts with
Emilie and Laura. These are the rubber bubbles
that we used.

March 24

Daddy and I walked around Morningside Park in the rain.
We were so tired of staying in the house. Mother is a little
better. Went to see "Oliver Twist." The man who played Fagin
was wonderfully good.

March 28

Went to the Senior play at Horace Mann.
It was William Gillette's "Secret Service."
They did very well. Mother said that the only way to pay for my
summer art class is to do the Vanderbilt wedding dresses.

April 2, 1912

Rained all day, but Laura and I were determined to skate rain or shine. All my friends have plans for the summer that do not include school. Laura is going to her summer cottage.

April 4

Went to see "Disraeli." The costumes were the most stylish I had ever seen. Afterward Mother took me to see an exhibition of ten American portrait painters.

April 6

Wore the new hat Mother made me to go shopping for some material to make my Spring dresses. Rode downtown on a bus. Fifth Avenue was crowded, a beautiful sight. Ah, it was a glorious day.

April 7

Daddy came home after ever such a long trip. His new friends had Sunday night tea with us and I made place cards. Everyone was amused.

April 8

My new spring dresses are growing, thanks
to Mother. She said I am not allowed to go to
Gloucester alone, which makes me think the art class will
be forbidden. Hurrying to get the Vanderbilt's baby book done.

April 10

The Vanderbilt baby came to visit last night. I presented
Mrs. Vanderbilt with my book and she enjoyed it. Mother has
agreed to do the Vanderbilt wedding, and she has
said I am <u>not</u> to feel guilty about it.

April 18

Emilie came over and spent the night. We illustrated a letter
to Mr. John Burroughs. The school is having an entertainment
in honor of his 75th birthday. He will give us a little talk.

John Burroughs...

was known as the Hudson River naturalist for his attention to the river valley north of New York
City. Burroughs (1837–1921) wrote essay after essay about details in the natural world — essays
collected into twenty-three volumes. Urging a return to nature, he was enormously popular even
as America was losing touch with nature and growing more industrialized and urban. By 1920
half of all Americans had moved to cities.

April 21

Went for a walk on Riverside with Daddy and saw the Columbia boys rowing. I do not know if I will ever go to a university like Columbia. Daddy always says girls have no need of college, unless they are from poor families and need to work as teachers.

April 22

Miss Dement read to us from a book called "Lives of the Artists." After class she asked me to make the cover for all of our letters to Mr. Burroughs. It is going to be a picture of the gateway to our campus.

April 27

Went up with Emilie to her home in Scarsdale. I am so glad she is my friend. We  gathered wild flowers and went to the horse show. Her horse won a blue ribbon. How lovely to have a horse of your own.

April 30

We are learning a very funny poem at school called "The Jumblies" by Edward Lear. Our class is going to sing and dance to it. I was still laughing in History and I got in trouble.

May 4, 1912

Mother has been very busy with the wedding. I hardly see her. She is so creative – the dresses are works of art. I see Nannie nearly every day.

May 9

As a present for the end of school coming up, Mother and Daddy have finally said I may go to the art class. Ah! It is going to be a glorious summer. But I must have a chaperone, so Mother will go with me. I hope she will not be bored or ill.

May 13

Was sent down from Nature Study class for talking with Emilie. She asked me to visit Virginia to meet her cousins over spring vacation. Now, how will I convince Mother to let me go without a chaperone?

May 14   Mother is stubborn, but I am as well.

Streets in New York, Part II

The streets began filling with cars in addition to the usual horses and carriages. Ford Model T's started coming out in 1908, and within a few years one million cars were on the road. The price kept dropping, and by 1912 a car cost about $400. The success of the car sparked an era when appliances (electric toasters, vacuum cleaners) that average people could afford were produced in factories in mass quantities. The first gas station in America opened in Pittsburgh in 1913. Up until then people had bought gas in stores along with the kerosene for their lamps. Besides gas stations, cars were about to usher in supermarkets, hotels, restaurants, and our contemporary consumer society.

May 15

Left for Virginia in the evening at 8:30 o'clock. As we drove down Broadway in a taxi cab it looked very pretty with all its electric signs and lights.

May 16

 In Virginia with Emilie. We took three baby chicks out of their incubator and taught them how to drink. Just darling little fluff balls. Went fishing with Jack and Alanson. I caught thirteen fish! One of the baby girls tried to make her hair like mine.

May 20

We played hide-and-seek. Fished and caught seven. We had a good laugh on Jack and Alanson for they stayed out a long time and caught about 150 crabs, but no fish. This must be what having brothers and sisters is like. It was good to see a place besides New York.

America was still growing...

with the induction of Arizona and New Mexico as states in 1912. America was now the fastest-growing country in history and the most prosperous, starting to distinguish itself as a confident leader. The population was still mainly rural, but it was migrating to cities. New York was especially bursting with people. It had already surpassed Paris and was catching up to London, then the world's most populous city.

May 21

Good-bye, Virginia. We hired an auto to drive us the fifteen miles to the station. Our chauffeur was a little black boy about twelve years old.

African Americans...

were struggling for equal rights. In 1909 the National Association for the Advancement of Colored People (N.A.A.C.P.) had been founded by a multiracial group of activists including W. E. B. Du Bois (1868–1963), the American civil-rights leader and author. Ahead of his time, Du Bois called for equality in all ways — economic, civil, and political. But for now, segregation was completely legal, from neighborhoods and schools to restaurants and drinking fountains. Especially in the South, racist "Jim Crow" laws ruled. Sixty-one black Americans are known to have been lynched in 1912. African Americans who left the South usually settled in Harlem, a section of upper Manhattan bordered roughly by 110th Street, the East River and Harlem River, 168th Street, Amsterdam Avenue, and Morningside Park. Harlem became the largest and most influential African-American community in the nation.

May 24

Went to the dentist. The dentist said that there was very little to do, but he wanted $500 for doing it. Mother talked about money problems again.

Modern dentistry…

had already been developed by 1912. Everything was in place — the electric drill, Novocain, porcelain and mercury fillings, X-rays, the special chair, and the dread. (General medical knowledge lagged far behind dental knowledge. In 1912 the average American man could expect to live to age 48, and woman to 51).

May 28

The school had a pageant out on the playgrounds. My group was dressed in three shades of yellow and represented the south wind. Beautiful. I painted the cover for the program. Not so beautiful.

May 29

School over today. I got my report card. Mother said it could be better. I wanted to go in Miss Hotchkiss' class next year. But I am going in Miss Roger's class instead. She does wear the most stylish hats.

June 7, 1912

It is too quiet. All my friends are away at camp or their summer homes. I have been sketching and packing. This weekend Mother and I are visiting cousins in Philadelphia. They have kittens.

June 9

In Philadelphia, playing
with darling kittens. We
visited historical places
and played on the see-
saw and swing in my
cousins' woods. Mother left today.
I get to go on the train all by myself.

Anne Elizabeth with relatives

June 10

Good-bye to Philadelphia. This was the first time I had ever
traveled alone. I quite enjoyed it. I am never bored when I
am alone.

June 12

Mother and I went for a walk. It was
not through a very good locality, and
the street was dirty, but we talked
about what to pack for Gloucester.

Streets in New York, Part III

The streets were filled with cars,
carriages — and dead creatures. In
1912 the Department of Health
reported having picked up 20,000
dead horses, mules, donkeys, and
cattle from city streets, as well as
nearly half a million smaller animals such as pigs, calves, and
sheep. Hundreds of thousands of
complaints came in about inade-
quate ventilation, leaking sewage,
unlicensed manure dumps, and
numerous other environmental
hazards.

June 16

Today is Mother's birthday. Daddy gave her some flowers.
I can not believe I forgot. I did not get her anything yet,
 but I am going to make her some
comic postcards.

June 17

To Brooklyn to visit Emilie's grandmother in the hospital. Emilie is
not as fond of her grandmother as I am of mine. The nurse took
us to see a tiny three-pound baby. It will be a miracle if it lives.

June 26

My birthday. I had a
very lovely one. Dinner
at the Arts Club with
Nannie. My birthday wish was to not make a fool of myself
at the art class next month.

June 29

Went to see an exhibition of beautiful lamp shades from
Germany. Came home and tried to make one
for Nannie. Counting the days until we leave.

June 30

My cousins in Philadelphia sent a telegram for my birthday. I thanked them for it in a letter with comic pictures of their kittens.

July 2, 1912

Went to see the dentist. He found quite a bit to be done. Conversation with Mother about money. Bought a new pair of shoes and had lunch at Cosmopolitan Club.

July 4

Today was a very sane Fourth. There were no firecrackers allowed within city limits. I am like a firecracker myself. Only six more days to go.

July 6

I am glad to say I went to the dentist for the last time. He kept me an hour and a half. There is nothing the least bit wrong with my teeth now.

July 7

On campus playing ball with Daddy. I almost bounced the ball into a baby carriage. Daddy promised to practice with me. I want to try out for basketball next year.

July 8

Went downtown shopping for a few last-minute things. I dread being apart from Daddy this summer, especially as he still does not really understand why I am going away.

July 9

Trying to help Mother pack. She has made such pretty clothes for me. But I have to choose carefully, lest our trunk sink the ship.

July 10

Started off to Gloucester by boat. Mother and I both hated to leave Daddy behind in hot old New York, but we had a lovely voyage.

July 11

We arrived in a horse and buggy. It was pouring rain, but we like our rooms. Met a few of the other girls. Everyone here is very stylish and they all love to draw.

July 12

Went down to the beach and sketched the people there. The water was blue and sparkling, and makes one glad to be alive. Mother saw Miss Nancy Walter and I am to start lessons tomorrow. Will I be able to wait?

July 13

Began lessons with Miss
Walter. She is not so very stylish,
but most encouraging. She told us to draw everything we see.
This is a little gate I can see from my window. The air is fresh
and heavenly here.

July 14

Took a long tramp around Eastern Point and came
home by those wonderful Bass Rocks. Everywhere
here is a bower of wild roses. Am having ever
such a good time. Already I hate for this summer to end.

July 15

This morning went up on the rocks with the class. While the
class painted the model, I painted the class.

July 16

I miss Daddy. Started a comical letter to
him. It is to be about a carrot and a
beet, as if they could have adventures.

July 22

No time to draw in my diary, or even to write. Am learning ever so much. Miss Walter said she has never had such a serious student. This is bliss.

July 24

Did a few little sketches on the beach, then went to the Hawthorne Inn for luncheon. Afterward I was introduced to the little girls there. I think I should like them if I knew them, but I am too busy with class.

July 26

Painted the model and went to Bass Rocks where I did a little watercolor of Mother. She is happy here as well, and even seems to approve of my art. I think she secretly wishes she was in our class.

July 28

Went for a car ride around Cape Ann and then to Pirate's Lane for a party for one of the teachers. The garden was hung with lanterns. Perhaps I will be a teacher someday. This is what women do.

July 29

We started to paint in Miss Walter's yard, but it rained and we had to go inside. I kept drawing while the others talked. We had a jolly time. All but the carpet who fared very badly with my ink.

August 2, 1912

Painting like mad every morning and every afternoon. Even when it rains. Then I paint on the porch. Am going to see some pictures of Gloucester fishing tonight. Class criticism tomorrow. I must be brave.

August 3

Criticism in the morning. Everyone was generous to me, even most of the other girls. In the afternoon had tea at Miss Walter's and she allowed me into her studio. I want to make great paintings like hers, but my own.

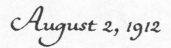

August 4

Went over to Bass Rocks to sketch the birds. But it was windy and cold, and as Mother had not packed me the proper wrap I could not stay.

August 5

Mother posed for the class and motored to Boston to visit a friend. I posed in the afternoon. With Mother gone I am more free.

August 7

Painted a model, a boy sitting on a dock. I had to sit on the ground which was wet, and I got a bad sore throat.

August 8

Feeling better. Everyone said I did the best painting so far today. A wonderful red-headed girl against some yellow dahlias. I wonder, could I stay here forever?

August 9

Mother is back, my chaperone. Miss Walter let me paint two models at the same time. It was windy and the canvas blew over three or four times. We took over supper to Miss Walter's and went for a glorious boat ride.

August 10

Mother saw Miss Walter and made an
arrangement. The class is ended for the other
girls, but I am going to go on alone. I am so pleased with
Mother. She is an artist too, only with needle and thread
instead of paint.

August 12

Painted Miss Bernstein on the rocks in back of Rocky Neck. A
gray dreary day, but I have the teachers and supplies all to
myself. The other girls left yesterday. Perhaps I will see some of
them next summer.

August 13

I love to draw hair, especially in the ocean breeze.
Painted a red-haired model in Miss Hallock's
yard. Her hair was very wonderful in
the sunshine.

August 14

Tried to paint Daddy from memory, but it was not good and
I rubbed it out. In the afternoon went to Gloucester Day with
Mother. Had a very nice time, but I do miss Daddy.
I saw this group of houses.

August 15

Miss Walter had me paint a clock, and then I posed for her.
She is doing a large canvas that is beautiful. But posing is not
nearly the fun of making my own paintings.

August 17

In the morning I painted Miss O'Heale while she
was painting. She has a tame canary. It will kiss
you. Kiss, kiss, ouch.

August 18

Made a picture to send to Daddy. Miss Walter has told me I could study with her next month back in the city. I was thrilled to find this out. It cheered me up on a cold rainy day.

August 21

Mother posed for me in the morning. Everybody seems to think it is the best picture I have done. This summer has been the finest in my life. Already I asked Mother if we can return next year. She would not say.

August 24

Good-bye to Gloucester. I will miss this place, and Miss Walter and the other teachers. Most of all I will miss making art every single day. There is a pure joy in it.

September 23, 1912

Start of school. I am turning over a new leaf. No more talking in class. Very good to see all the girls again. Especially Emilie, but we did <u>not</u> get in trouble for talking. Miss Rogers indeed had the prettiest hat of all. And my Miss Pratt is back from Egypt.

September 24

Daddy and I were all alone for supper and it seemed very nice. He looked at my work from the summer but did not praise overmuch. Nor did Nannie when she saw it. I fear no one understands.

September 26

Took a long walk with Daddy and Miss Robbins, our upstairs neighbor. The woods are perfect at this time of year. Went to the moving pictures with Emilie. She was polite about my new paintings.

September 28

No more piano lessons, thank you. Started up private art lessons with Miss Walter. She praises my work as much as Miss Pratt. Mother took me to the campus and went off to shop, while I drew and drew.

Movies...

were entertainment nearly everyone could afford — a ticket cost just 5 cents — and millions of Americans were going daily. Recent films Anne Elizabeth might have seen were *A Tale of Two Cities* starring Norma Talmadge, *Queen Elizabeth* starring the dramatic Sarah Bernhardt, *An Unseen Enemy* starring Lillian Gish, *The Musketeers of Pig Alley,* and *The New York Hat* starring popular Mary Pickford (the latter three films were directed by the legendary D. W. Griffith).

October 4, 1912

Had a basketball game. I want to play guard on Laura's team. I have that place so far but the teams are not chosen. The boys come around to tease.

Girls in sports...

were still a controversial idea. Proper attire was an issue. In 1910 an Australian woman was arrested for swimming in Boston Harbor in an "indecent" one-piece swimsuit (it exposed her legs). Even baby girls were required to wear complete bathing costumes. In 1914 the American Olympic Committee opposed women's competition in the Olympics. The only exception was the floor exercise, where women were required to wear long skirts.

October 5

Tried on dresses. Mother is making me a brown serge middy blouse suit, a green dress, and two white dresses for dancing school. I shall be the most stylish girl in Morningside. Practiced basketball with Daddy.

October 10

Stayed for hours after school. Not for punishment. Miss Rogers and four of the teachers had me color maps of Europe for the different rooms.

World geography...

was becoming important to know. This year, 1912, war broke out in the Balkans. Montenegro declared war on Turkey. Bulgaria and Serbia mobilized their armies. Rivalries deepened among Germany, France, Great Britain, Russia, and Austria-Hungary. Germany, trumpeting its superiority, renewed its alliances with Italy and Austria. In 1914 the Archduke Francis Ferdinand, heir to the throne of Austria, would be assassinated, setting off World War I. The United States would try to stay neutral, but in 1915 a German submarine would sink a British ship called the *Lusitania*, killing Americans. America entered the war in 1917 with the stated purpose of "making the world safe for democracy."

October 12

Miss Rogers was absent this morning and left word for me to keep the class busy drawing. Started to make paper lamp shades for Nannie.

Anne Elizabeth, reader

October 14

Went to the library and returned "The Lady of the Aroostook" which I enjoyed ever so much. Took out "A Chance Acquaintance." Lesson with Miss Walter, who is so splendid about my art that it inspires me.

Libraries...

were a hot topic in the early twentieth century. Many believed that New York required a great library free to everyone if it was to be a world-class city. Finally, in 1911, the New York Public Library opened, a magnificent marble building on Fifth Avenue with majestic stone lions guarding the doors. Some 40,000 people visited on the very first day, roaming the seventy-five miles of shelves.

The Morningside Branch didn't open until 1914, so Anne Elizabeth perhaps used the 115th Street Branch, a three-story landmark building. Over the course of this year she mentions numerous books — these two here are comic novels by American writer William Dean Howells from the 1870s. Recently published books that she could have read were L. Frank Baum's *The Wonderful Wizard of Oz*, Francis Hodgson Burnett's *The Secret Garden*, L. M. Montgomery's *Anne of Green Gables*, Jack London's *Call of the Wild*, Baroness Orczy's *The Scarlet Pimpernel*, and Edith Nesbit's *Five Children and It*.

One woman artist Anne Elizabeth may have encountered in her reading was Beatrix Potter, creator of the popular Peter Rabbit series for children. These books had been appearing since 1902. A botanist, Potter started out by illustrating her letters to children — with pale pen-and-ink drawings that may have influenced Anne Elizabeth's.

School…

was sometimes a luxury. Only one-third of American children were in elementary school at this time, with less than ten percent graduating from high school. Instead, many children as young as Anne Elizabeth had to work. There were no laws against it. Children were cheaper to hire than adults; they worked twelve-hour days in factories, coal mines, and textile mills, and they didn't complain as much about unsafe conditions and terrible pay. The plight of working children was just coming to light. With the establishment this year of the U.S. Children's Bureau, intended to prevent the abuse of children, the movement to ban child labor began.

October 15

Tried to work in charcoal and rather made a mess of it. This afternoon I got acquainted with Hildaguard Noss. She seems to be a lovely little girl.

October 17

Seventh grade is very much harder than last year. I like all my classes, but I have scarce time to myself. To make art, I am going to have to push myself because no one else will.

October 19

Miss Walter tells me to train my eyes by looking closely at nature, people, the neighborhood. Even hats. She said this is how one becomes an artist.

October 21

Went with Mother to Folsom and Macbeths galleries downtown and saw a wonderful little Vermeer at Knordlers. The more art I see, the more it fills my mind. But I did not say this to Mother.

October 22

Went downtown with Mother to hunt for a corset for me. We finally had to order one. It is much too embarrassing to draw.

October 23

Daddy took me to the Hippodrome. We had ice cream and a fine time. Except he said that I am taking my studies too seriously. He says he does not get to see me often enough.

Underwear of the day...

was often cumbersome, even painful. The corset, an unhealthy device made of whalebones and steel rods, was designed to squeeze women into an hourglass shape. Girls as young as six wore "training corsets," with the real thing being required by age fourteen. Not until 1913 did the first modern brassiere come into being, and not until the introduction of elastic did the bra dethrone the corset.

October 24

Nannie came over and I gave her the lamp shades I made. I walked her to her carriage. She does not understand why I like art so much, but she promised to help me go to Gloucester next summer, if Mother says no.

The Hippodrome...

was yet another form of entertainment in an era with no TV or computers. Stretching an entire block near Times Square, it was a grand, high-tech palace where you could see movies, circus acts, performances by escape artist Harry Houdini, and shows that were overwhelming spectacles. Early shows like "A Yankee Circus on Mars" combined vaudeville, pantomime, dance, technological novelties, hundreds of chorus girls, elephant parades, and dancing horses. The theater could seat more than five thousand, and tickets cost less than a dollar. The Hippodrome was inspired by another development, the department store. These gigantic stores promoted shopping as an important and entertaining activity for all classes.

Election Day...

was coming up — the fourth of November. Democrat Woodrow Wilson from nearby New Jersey became the twenty-eighth president. All this year, an exciting four-way race had been taking place. The current president, William Taft, had been running for re-election. Popular former president Theodore Roosevelt, another Republican, came back from his African safari and didn't like how Taft was doing. "My hat is in the ring," TR — as he was affectionately nicknamed — announced, even though he had promised not to run for a third term (he should have said third *consecutive* term). Taft won the Republican nomination, so TR ran as a Progressive (Bull Moose) Republican. This was the first national political party to support women's suffrage. It also called for the prohibition of child labor and a minimum wage for women. The fourth candidate was Eugene Debs of the Socialist Party. He got 6 percent of the vote. Roosevelt got 27 percent and Taft got 23 percent, splitting the Republican vote, which meant Wilson won easily with 42 percent. Wilson wanted America to stay out of foreign wars and was firmly opposed to women voting (even though he treated his second wife, Edith, as an equal partner). On both matters, he found it useful to change his mind later.

October 26

As no one in our class was absent last week, we had a reward of getting out half an hour early. Emilie came home to lunch with me. She is a fine friend, but not very ambitious.

October 28

I told Miss Pratt about this diary, even about the drawings which I no longer have much time to make. Now she and Miss Rogers have asked me to write a sort of diary for the whole school. A list of events, with drawings to match. I was thrilled, though now I will have less time than ever.

November 4, 1912

Mother has headaches again. I read aloud to her most of this afternoon. Then I went to dancing school. Dancing does not come so easily to me.

November 6.

Went to see an exhibition of Miss Walter's things at the Macdowell Club. She told me about a proper art school I might go to, right here in the city. It is the same one Mr. Seton went to.

November 7

Mother is ill in bed and I kept busy with the school diary. She said I am allowed to do the diary for Horace Mann as long as my grades are good. She sat up for a little while and put my hair into braids.

The Art Students League of New York...

is where most of the well-known artists in America have either taught or studied. It was founded *by* artists *for* artists in 1875. Afternoons were reserved for women, evenings for men, with tuition at $5 a month. The most demanding class was life drawing, and the League's class was the only one available to women in New York at the time. Artists associated with the League include Romare Bearden, Thomas Hart Benton, Isabel Bishop, Alexander Calder, George Grosz, Roy Lichtenstein, Louise Nevelson, Georgia O'Keeffe, Jackson Pollock, Mark Rothko, and John Sloan — who once painted *Rector's Daughter*, a portrait of Anne Elizabeth. Today the League, located on West 57th Street, nurtures some 2,000 students from around the world in drawing, painting, and sculpture.

November 9

Miss Pratt asked me to teach some of the younger girls during her absence today. I tried to show them how to do a scene from a fairy tale. I do not think I can explain to others how to draw. It frustrates me.

November 15

In the evening Mother and Daddy started to teach me bridge but we were interrupted by their friends who spent the evening. I amused myself drawing tiny people.

November 23

Mother has been ill again for days. No one knows what is wrong. Daddy took me to see "Fanny's First Play." I do not know when I have enjoyed a play so much.

December 4, 1912

Mother is better. Daddy took Emilie and me to the Bronx to see the zoo. I wanted to sketch each animal, but Daddy had to hurry home.

December 7

Worked in charcoal at art school. Miss Walter thinks it is the best I have done. Daddy still hasn't found time to teach me chess, but I am finally playing bridge. We are going to play every Saturday night.

December 10

Went to dancing school. The boy called Tom is the only one that can dance. Wore one of my new white dresses to swirl around the room.

An older Anne, in costume

December 12

Skating with Emilie. Lovely! The first time I had been on ice this year. I am starved for free time. Emilie has all the free time one could want.

December 14

Worked all afternoon on lessons. Hunting out synonyms in the dictionary. Mother helped me with my French. I do hope I will get to Paris someday. Everyone says it is magic for artists.

December 15

Nannie came to supper. Her friend Mr. Huxlbeut wants us to come up to Lake Placid next summer and share his cottage. Now I am worried. I wanted to paint with Miss Walter in Gloucester.

December 18

To the 119th Street rink with Laura and Mary. It was the first time they had been on outdoor ice. They do not understand why I am always busy with art class. They are not serious about things.

December 19

Painted a hairy old man at art school. He said, "If you keep on like that, you'll get somewhere or other some day." I think he meant it. I wonder where I will get to.

December 20

Tremendously windy day. Trying to Christmas shop. In the evening I went to hear "The Magic Flute" with Miss Pratt, still my favorite teacher.

December 25

Merry Christmas to Mother, Daddy, Nannie, my friends, the best teachers in the world, Miss Pratt and Miss Walter, and even to the hairy old man at art school.

And to myself – Anne Elizabeth Rector, artist.

What Happened Next?

Anne Elizabeth did go on to graduate from Horace Mann School, with honors. A college for women, Vassar College in Poughkeepsie (open since 1861), offered her a scholarship. Her parents were surprised and impressed. But she turned down the offer. By now, she knew she really wanted to focus on her art.

The year of this diary seems to have been the turning point for her. This is when she started to dream that art might become her life — a bold move for a girl of her time and place. Her parents took it for granted that their daughter was artistic — it was nothing extraordinary. They believed her real role was to marry someone respectable and have children.

Anne Elizabeth as an adult

Instead, with her flair for independence, she enrolled in the Art Students League of New York.

Over the next few years, Anne Elizabeth became an accomplished painter. She planned a whole life as a fine artist, expressing herself through art. She didn't have to worry about support — income from family investments wasn't great, but it was enough to live on. Eventually she went abroad to study in Paris, a heavenly city for artists. She married a fellow art student, Edmund Duffy, and they moved from Paris to Baltimore, Maryland, in 1923. Success as a female painter would have been unlikely for her times, but Anne Elizabeth was well on her way.

Then, in 1929, the stock market crashed. It brought financial ruin to many Americans, and Anne Elizabeth's family lost what investments they had. Her focus changed. Earning money was now the priority. She began commuting to New York and collaborating with her mother on art they could get paid for — painting small boxes, making unique toys, building elaborate dollhouses. She branched out into furniture handmade for the rich and famous, like movie star Carole Lombard.

At this she became a huge success. Admirers who thought she could draw like an angel were

Anne and her husband, Edmund Duffy (standing, with scarf)

dismayed that hard times forced her to switch from "art for art's sake" to "art for money's sake." But Anne Elizabeth didn't look back. Ultimately she took on the role of glamorous, independent businesswoman, using her creativity to support her parents as well as her own family. A pioneering woman in a mostly all-male

Anne Elizabeth with her daughter, Sara Anne

world, she took care of everyone around her in great style.

She was a supportive wife to Duffy, who went on to become a political cartoonist for the *Baltimore Sun,* working closely with H. L. Mencken, famed writer and journalist. Duffy won the Pulitzer Prize three times for his cartoons.

In her mid-thirties, she had a daughter, Sara Anne. Anne Elizabeth made her the most lavish dollhouse imaginable, as well as little books, clothes, and dance dresses to die for. A paper-doll lover in her own childhood, she made dozens of exquisite dolls for Sara Anne. But daily child care was not her style, and she sent Sara Anne off to boarding school at age ten.

Some of the paper dolls Anne Elizabeth made

With her spare time, Anne Elizabeth cooked gourmet meals, made her own chocolates, designed and sewed extraordinary clothes for herself and her family, and was an artist in all that she did.

Whenever she had money to spare, she invested in real estate. She was a very wealthy woman when she died in 1970. She left her vast collection of prints to the Cooper-Hewitt Museum in New York.

Some of Anne Elizabeth's art as an adult. These figures show the influence Beatrix Potter may have had on her art style.

It included a portfolio of bird paintings by John James Audubon, which if left intact would have been worth $1 million. But they were more useful to Anne as art supplies, and she had cut them up for collages.

It never seemed to occur to her to share this diary with others. No one even knew it existed until her daughter, Sara Anne, found it in the attic while sorting through her late mother's things. Almost everything in it surprised Sara Anne. Anne Elizabeth had cultivated a "tough as nails" image and never let her guard down or spoke of doubts, fears, or loneliness. She seldom talked about her own childhood and *never* conveyed that it was anything less than perfect.

Anne Elizabeth, businesswoman

Anne Elizabeth's family has long wanted to share this diary, with its charming drawings, to readers of today, offering them a slice of life in 1912 New York.

Anne Elizabeth at work

A Note from Anne Elizabeth's Granddaughter

My grandmother, Anne Elizabeth, was twelve years old when she kept this diary. I was twelve years old when my grandmother died. As I sit down to write this, my oldest daughter is twelve. Anne Elizabeth was an only child. Her daughter, Sara Anne, was an only child. Sara Anne, my mother, had three daughters: me, and my sisters, Sasha and Maro. I have two girls, Loulou and Fanny.

It's funny, when I sit down to write this note I find I have only sporadic memories. I remember sleepovers with my grandmother, when we would have shrimp soup and mushroom sandwiches for dinner. Extra place settings were laid out for my two imaginary friends. There were always paper dolls, lots of paper dolls. Elaborate doll houses, bunnies, and mice families. Grandmother would make paper dolls of our family, but also of the president and his family. There is an awful lot that I don't remember. She liked to watch a game show called Password on television – and she always won. In my memory, she could do crossword puzzles as fast as you could write the letters in the boxes.

My mother kept very few things of Anne Elizabeth's. There are not a lot of photographs or drawings or furniture or the silk flowers she made. But my mother did keep Anne Elizabeth's diary and a few scattered paper-doll families. They are treasures. Her exquisite drawings, her delicate handwriting, are unique. I didn't know this little girl, who loved spelling, new clothes, and ice skating. But I do remember her. And now, almost one hundred years later, I have two girls. One loves spelling, one ice skating, and they both love new clothes.

Catherine Chermayeff
June 2003

Some Tips on Keeping a Diary

by Kathleen Krull

- ◆ Ask for a diary or journal for your next birthday. A birthday is a good time to start (so is the first day of school or New Year's Day) — you're already thinking about yourself more than usual.

- ◆ Unlike other areas of your life, this is one place where *you* are the boss. You decide what goes in and when and in how much detail. You rule. Make the most of it.

- ◆ Don't worry if you skip a few days, or weeks, or months. Anne Elizabeth's book commanded her to write every day (*"Nulla dies sine linea"*—Latin for "No day without a line"), but no one is perfect. The important thing is not to give up.

- ◆ Not all of us are as talented as Anne Elizabeth, but we all have our own artistic style. Try to develop it by illustrating things in your life as well as writing them down. Even if your drawings look weird, they will give you many laughs in the future.

- ◆ Please add emotion to your diary, for your own sake as well as for your future biographers. If you only list events, you will bore even yourself later. Tell how you feel about what is going on in your life. When I reread my sixth-grade diary, seeing the word "HILARIOUS!" brings back to me all the giddiness and astonishment of that moment.

❖ On the day John F. Kennedy was assassinated, I wrote about fluff in my diary, even though I was very shaken by the event. Try to write about your life *and times*. As fascinating as you are, break away for world or national events once in a while. During a presidential campaign, for instance, what do *you* think of the candidates? You will be glad later to know your reactions to current events.

❖ If you are thinking about being a writer or an artist, keeping a diary is the single best thing you can do to develop your powers. It is extremely valuable no matter what you hope to become.

❖ Be honest. Read *Harriet the Spy* by Louise Fitzhugh (if you haven't already) for inspiration. Be inquisitive. Outrageous. Tell secrets. This is how you find out who you are.

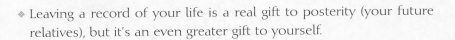

❖ Do keep your diary in a safe place away from snoops. If your siblings find out you are keeping a diary, they will want to read it, guaranteed.

❖ Leaving a record of your life is a real gift to posterity (your future relatives), but it's an even greater gift to yourself.

Index

Author's Note

All drawings and all events are taken directly from Anne Elizabeth's 1912 diary. The volume was brought to the attention of Little, Brown by her granddaughter, Catherine Chermayeff.

Anne Elizabeth was raised to believe a lady should not show feelings, and it wasn't her nature to reveal how she felt about her daily activities. While trying to stay true to her spirit, I added interpretations, continuity, and emotion. I based this extra information on interviews with her daughter, Sara Anne Chermayeff, and her granddaughter, Catherine — both of whom are artists in New York City. To create a context, I also added historical details, which come from:

- The Art Students League of New York, www.theartstudentsleague.org.

- Degregoria, William. *The Complete Book of U.S. Presidents.* NY: Wings Books, 1993.

- Ecology Hall of Fame: John Burroughs, www.ecotopia.org/ehof/burroughs.

- Gloucester, Massachusetts, www.gloucesterma.com.

- Granfield, Linda. *97 Orchard Street, New York: Stories of Immigrant Life.* NY: Tundra Books, 2001.

- Grun, Bernard. *The Timetables of History: A Horizontal Linkage of People and Events.* NY: Touchstone Books, 1991.

- Hakim, Joy. *A History of US, Vol. 8, An Age of Extremes.* NY: Oxford, 1994.

- The Horace Mann School, www.horacemann.org.

- Internet Broadway Database, www.ibdb.com.

- Morningside Heights, www.morningside-heights.net.

- New York Public Library: History, www.nypl.org/admin/pro/history.html.

- Teachers College Columbia University: Facts, www.tc.columbia.edu/abouttc/tcfacts.htm.

- Timeline of Costume History: 20th Century Western costume: 1910–1920, www.costumes.org/pages/timelinepages/timeline.htm.

- Trager, James. *The Women's Chronology: A Year-by-Year Record, from Prehistory to the Present.* NY: Holt, 1994.

I am most grateful to Sheila Cole for her help with this book — and also to editors Alvina Ling and Megan Tingley.

— Kathleen Krull